D1307317

Where do bats sleep?

Contents

Where did the hamburger get its name?

Where do butterflies come from?

Butterflies have four parts to their lives. They hatch from tiny eggs. Then they become little, wormlike animals called *caterpillars*. They spend their days eating plants and growing. One day caterpillars stop eating. They spin a belt of silk and tie themselves to a twig. This hardens and is called a *pupa* or *chrysalis*. Inside, the caterpillar begins to transform. After many weeks, a new butterfly breaks free. When its wings dry, it can fly.

FUN FACT

You might not see Monarch butterflies year-round: That's because they *migrate* and spend the winter along the coast of California or in warm and sunny Mexico. In spring they return to areas across the United States.

KIDS ASK™

Where?

Illustrations by Anne Kennedy

Publications International, Ltd.

Where do butterflies come from?

Where does honey come from?

Bees make honey to store as food during the winter. To make honey, bees collect *nectar* from flowers and plants and carry it back to the hive. At the hive, worker bees store the nectar in wax chambers. They add *enzymes,* which change the nectar to honey. A hive full of bees only needs about 20 to 30 pounds of honey to survive the winter. The rest can be harvested by humans.

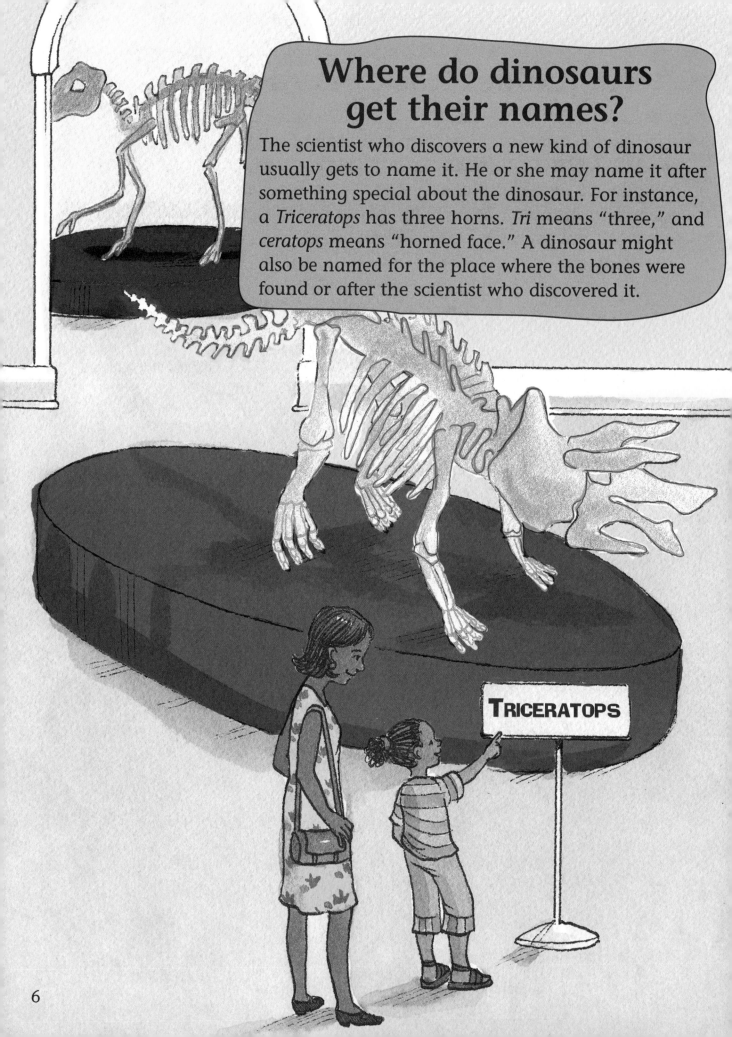

Where do dinosaurs get their names?

The scientist who discovers a new kind of dinosaur usually gets to name it. He or she may name it after something special about the dinosaur. For instance, a *Triceratops* has three horns. *Tri* means "three," and *ceratops* means "horned face." A dinosaur might also be named for the place where the bones were found or after the scientist who discovered it.

TRICERATOPS

Where did all the dinosaurs go?

Scientists don't really know why there are no dinosaurs today. They became *extinct,* or died out, about 65 million years ago. One reason may be that the earth became colder, and the plants and animals that the dinosaurs ate died. When a dinosaur had nothing to eat, it died too.

TYRANNOSAURUS REX

FUN FACT

Tyrannosaurus rex could eat 500 pounds of meat in one bite. That equals more than 1,000 hamburgers!

Where do caves come from?

Caves are made from soft rock. Over thousands of years, rainwater soaks the ground and drips down through small holes in the rock. Slowly, the rock is worn down, and a hollow cave is formed.

Where do bats sleep?

Bats sleep during the day in caves, hollow trees, or cracks in rocks. Their favorite place is a cave. Thousands of bats sleep hanging upside down. Their back feet have strong claws that allow them to hang from the ceiling. Bats sleep close together and wrap their wings around their bodies to keep warm.

FUN FACT

In some caves, water runs along the ceiling. As it drops down to the cave floor, it carries with it some of the *minerals* from the rock. Over time, the water escapes into the air, but the minerals do not. The minerals are left behind and form *stalactites*, which look like icicles made of stone.

Where do bananas grow?

Bananas grow on *plantations,* or farms, in countries with lots of sunshine and rain. These countries are near the *equator,* where it is hot all year. Banana plants are not actually trees: They have large, soft, overlapping leaves. These plants can grow up to 30 feet tall. They are the tallest plants that don't have woody stems or trunks.

Bananas 40¢ per lb.

Locally Grown

FUN FACT

Even though Iceland is far from the equator, bananas are grown in hothouses all over the country.

Where does chocolate come from?

Chocolate comes from the *cacao* tree. This kind of tree only grows in places that are hot all year long. Big pods grow from the trunk. Inside the pods are seeds. These seeds are the cocoa beans from which chocolate is made. The beans are dried, then shipped to other countries where they are made into chocolate foods.

11

Where is the Statue of Liberty?

The Statue of Liberty stands on a pedestal in New York Harbor in New York City. She was made in France and given to the United States in 1886 as a symbol of the friendship between the two countries. Today, people think of freedom, independence, and opportunity when they see her.

Where do the colors in fireworks come from?

When fireworks shoot into the sky, they explode. The explosion burns *minerals.* This makes the bright colors you see just before hearing the loud bang. Different minerals make different colors: Some burn green, some deep red, and some bright yellow. Copper, which is the mineral on the outside of pennies, makes blue fireworks. Colors such as orange, white, lavender, and gold are made by combining minerals.

FUN FACT

The Declaration of Independence was adopted on July 4, 1776. By the early 1800s, parades, picnics, and fireworks became part of the annual Fourth of July celebration.

10:00 Math

10:30 Reading

$$3 \quad 2$$
$$+3 \quad +4$$

Where does chalk come from?

Natural chalk is a type of soft white *limestone*. Limestone is a type of rock that was created when the shells of ancient ocean animals were crushed together over millions of years. However, the chalk you use at school or on the sidewalk is not made from limestone. It is made from a mineral called *gypsum*, which is very soft and fine-grained.

Aa Bb Cc Dd Ee Ff Gg Hh Ii Jj Kk Ll Mm

Where did the alphabet come from?

An alphabet is a set of symbols, called *letters*, that represent the sounds used in spoken language. The *Phoenicians* were the first people to create an alphabet. They lived about 3,000 years ago in parts of Africa, Asia, and Europe surrounding the Mediterranean Sea. Their alphabet had just 22 letters. English is written in the Latin alphabet, which has 26 letters.

FUN FACT

The word "alphabet" comes from the names of the first two letters of the Greek alphabet, *alpha* and *beta*.

α β

Where did the moon come from?

Scientists have many *theories,* or ideas, about where the moon came from. One is that the earth was hit by a rock the size of a small planet billions of years ago. The force was so great that a chunk of our planet broke off and formed the moon.

Where does the sun go when it sets?

Each day the earth spins around one time. As the earth spins, one side of it faces the sun. On that side of the earth it is daytime. On the side that faces away from the sun it is nighttime. The sun is always shining, but when your side of the earth spins away from the sun you cannot see it.

Where were French fries invented?

French fries first appeared in Paris in the 1840s. The French called them "fried potatoes." Thomas Jefferson tried these fried potatoes when he was in Paris, and he had his chef make them when he returned to America. Americans called them "French fried potatoes," and they were very popular. In the 1930s, people started calling them simply "French fries."

Where did the hamburger get its name?

Is there ham in hamburgers? No! The usual hamburger you get in a restaurant is made of beef, which comes from a cow. Hamburgers are actually named after a town in Germany called Hamburg. They were once known as "Hamburg steaks." Hamburger patties were made for quite some time before anyone thought to serve them on a bun.

FUN FACT

Hot dogs are a type of sausage that was first called a frankfurter, or "frank." They got the name "hot dog" when a cartoonist drew a frankfurter as a dachshund dog on a bun!

Where does sand come from?

Sand is really little bits of rock. Wind and water break rocks down into tiny pieces over time. Different types of sand are created from different types of rock. For example, black sand comes from volcanic rock. Some types of sand are made from coral, shells, or bones that have broken down into fine bits over millions of years.

Where does a cactus get water to grow?

Most cacti grow in hot, dry deserts. There is not much rain in the desert, so cacti have had to *adapt,* or change, to survive. Cacti have roots that spread out along the surface of the ground. That way, when it does rain, they can quickly soak up the water as soon as it seeps into the sand. While it's raining, cacti grow many tiny roots from their main roots to soak up more water quickly. When it stops raining, these little roots die off so the cactus can save energy until the next rainfall.

FUN FACT

Roadrunners can run up to 15 miles per hour, fast enough to catch a rattlesnake.

Where does garbage go?

Usually, a garbage truck comes to collect all the garbage set on curbs or in trash containers in the neighborhood. Then the garbage from these trucks is transferred to a larger truck. This giant trailer truck takes the garbage to a *landfill*, where the garbage will eventually be buried.

FUN FACT

Recycling just one soda can saves enough energy to run your television for three hours!

Where do cats' claws go when they're not out?

Cats have a claw on each toe. But you can't see the claws until they are used to scratch something. When a cat doesn't need its claws, its toes are bent. The claws are pulled back under the skin on the toes. When the cat needs its claws, the toes straighten and the claws are pushed out. If the claws were always out, they would lose their sharpness from the cat walking on them.

Where do parrots learn to talk?

A wild parrot would never say, "Hello," or "Polly want a cracker?" Talking parrots learn these words from people. They don't actually know what the words mean. Instead they learn to *mimic*, or copy, the sounds around them. Most parrots require lots of attention to learn to talk.

FUN FACT

African Gray parrots are the kings of talkers. Some of these parrots have been known to repeat lines of songs or plays. The most famous Gray parrot had a vocabulary of nearly 1,000 words!

Where do birds sleep?

Birds are light sleepers. Some rest together in a *flock* with a few birds looking out for danger while the others catnap. When birds sleep, they usually fluff up their feathers to keep warm. Most sleep standing or sitting. Some birds sleep with their head turned resting on their shoulder and bill tucked under their wing.

Where do fireflies get their light?

Fireflies have chemicals in their bodies that allow them to glow. The glow is caused by air coming into their bodies and reacting with these chemicals. When the air is used up, the glow fades. Fireflies can control their flashing. When it's warmer outside, the fireflies' flashing patterns are faster.

FUN FACT

When a bullfrog croaks, the sound is made by the vocal cords in the throat, but the sound is projected out its ears!

Where do escalator steps go?

The steps of an escalator form when they come out of the floor. The steps are really a big, motor-driven belt moving around two rollers. Under the floor, the belt is flat. As the belt comes out of the floor, it gradually becomes steps. At the top and bottom, the steps flatten out. This helps people get ready to step off.

FUN FACT

The longest escalator in North America is in the CNN Center in Atlanta, Georgia. It's 160 feet tall, which would take you to the top of a Douglas fir tree—nearly eight stories off the ground!

Where does rain come from?

Clouds are made of tiny water droplets. When the air in the sky cools, the droplets cling together and get bigger. At last, they become too heavy to stay in the sky, and they fall. It's raining!

Where do rivers begin?

Many rivers begin as small mountain streams made of melted snow and fresh rainwater. As the stream travels downhill, it is joined by other streams. It grows and grows until it becomes a big river.

FUN FACT

About 80 percent of the earth is covered by water, but only about 1 percent of the water is safe to drink.

Where do birds go in winter?

Some birds stay in one area year-round. Others, however, move toward warmer areas near the equator in the winter. In the spring, they fly back to where they came from. This is called *migration*. Many birds migrate long distances. Canada geese travel the length of the North American continent. Groups of geese fly in a wedge-shape formation, honking as they go.